THE CHRISTIAN YEAR

HELEN ◇ *ADAMS*

ILLUSTRATIONS BY
JANE REYNOLDS

Hunt & Thorpe

Scripture quotations are from
the Holy Bible: New International Version.

Helen Steiner Rice poem on back cover
reprinted with permission by Helen Steiner
Rice Foundation.

PICTURE ACKNOWLEDGMENTS
Jane Reynolds: cover, p. 3, 6-7, 17, 18-19, 26, 30, 38, 43, 46,
50, 58-59, 61, 65, 70, 78, 84, 88, 91, 95, 98-99, 101, 105, 110, 115,
117, 119, 123; Rowland Antony: p. 21, 51, 86, 87. Russ Busby
(photo): p. 13; Dallas Baptist University (photo): p. 127;
Mary Evans Picture Library: p. 9; The Mansell
Collection: p. 56.

A CIP catalogue record for this book is available
from the British Library.

Manufactured in Singapore.

INTRODUCTION

The passing of the year can bring
great sadness and great joy. But we have the comfort
that Spring follows Winter, that the sun always returns.

As Christians we have the blessing
of the Resurrection and the certainty of
the coming again of Christ. Throughout the year
we can draw strength from his life as it is remembered
in the Church year. The great chapter eleven of Hebrews
encourages us to remember the saints, and the collective
experiences of the saints down the ages is God's gift
to us – they point us to Christ.

Dates can be helpful reminders of what we know,
and prompters of what we can look forward to.
It is my hope that this little book will lighten your path
in the year to come.

JANUARY

January 1

As the three astronauts of Apollo 8, Lovell, Anders and Borman, circled the moon they read back to those watching them and listening to them on "good earth" these words from Genesis, chapter one.

"In the beginning God created the heaven and the earth. And the earth was without form, and void; and darkness was upon the face of the deep. And the Spirit of God moved upon the face of the waters. And God said, 'Let there be light:' and there was light. And God saw the light, that it was good."

January 2

I've often taken comfort from these verses in which God says to Joshua, "Have I not commanded you? Be strong and courageous. Do not be terrified; do not be discouraged, for the Lord your God will be with you wherever you go."

Joshua 1:9

January 3

"Humility is not a mere ornament of a Christian, but an essential part of the new creature. It is a contradiction to be a true Christian and not humble. All that will be Christians must be Christ's disciples and come to him to learn, and their lesson is to be 'meek and lowly.'"

Richard Baxter

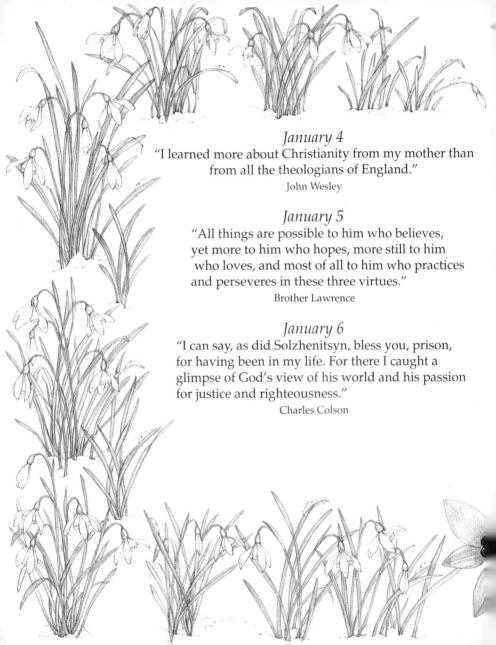

January 4

"I learned more about Christianity from my mother than from all the theologians of England."

John Wesley

January 5

"All things are possible to him who believes, yet more to him who hopes, more still to him who loves, and most of all to him who practices and perseveres in these three virtues."

Brother Lawrence

January 6

"I can say, as did Solzhenitsyn, bless you, prison, for having been in my life. For there I caught a glimpse of God's view of his world and his passion for justice and righteousness."

Charles Colson

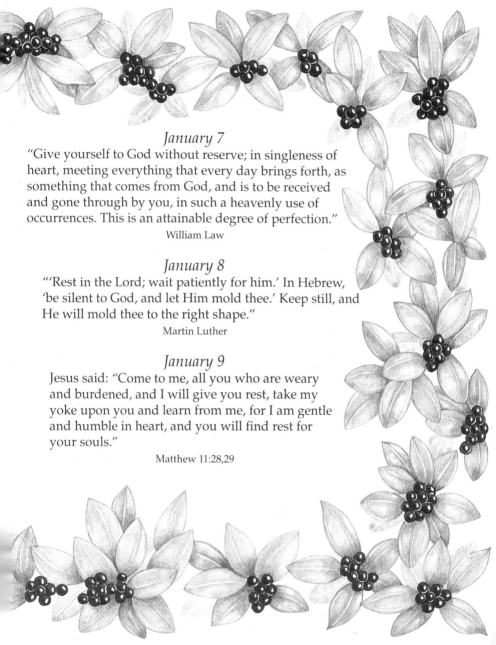

January 7

"Give yourself to God without reserve; in singleness of heart, meeting everything that every day brings forth, as something that comes from God, and is to be received and gone through by you, in such a heavenly use of occurrences. This is an attainable degree of perfection."

William Law

January 8

"'Rest in the Lord; wait patiently for him.' In Hebrew, 'be silent to God, and let Him mold thee.' Keep still, and He will mold thee to the right shape."

Martin Luther

January 9

Jesus said: "Come to me, all you who are weary and burdened, and I will give you rest, take my yoke upon you and learn from me, for I am gentle and humble in heart, and you will find rest for your souls."

Matthew 11:28,29

January 10

In a lecture in 1948 Dr. Albert Einstein said:
"The true problem lies in the hearts and thoughts of men. It is not a physical but an ethical one... What terrifies us is not the explosive force of the atomic bomb, but the power of the wickedness of the human heart."

January 11

The apostle Paul suffered hardship and beatings and mocking more than most at the hands of evil men and yet he could still write:

"We know that in all things God works for the good of those who love him, who have been called according to his purpose."

Romans 8:28

January 12

"Jesus Christ taught men the simple truth about themselves: that they were selfish; enslaved to their appetites; blind, sick, unhappy, sinners; that it was laid upon Himself to deliver, enlighten, bless, and heal them; and that this would be brought about by hatred of self, and by following him through poverty to the death of the Cross."

Pascal

January 13

"He who believes in
God is not careful for
the morrow, but labors
joyfully and with a
great heart. 'For He
giveth His beloved, as in
sleep.' They must work
and watch, yet never be
careful or anxious, but
commit all to him, and live in
serene tranquillity; with a quiet heart, as one who
sleeps safely and quietly."

Martin Luther

January 14

"It is no great matter to associate with the good and gentle,
for this is naturally pleasing to all, and every one happily
enjoys peace, and loves those which do not agree with him.
But to be able to live in peace with hard and perverse
persons is a great grace, and a most commendable thing."

Thomas à Kempis

January 15

"If anyone says, 'I love God,' yet hates his brother, he
is a liar. For anyone who does not love his brother,
whom he has seen, cannot love God, whom he has
not seen. And he has given us this command:
'Whoever loves God must also love his brother.'"

1 John 4:19–21

January 16

God moves in a mysterious way,
His wonders to perform;
He plants his footsteps in the sea,
And rides upon the storm.

Deep in unfathomable mines
Of never-failing skill
He treasures up his bright designs,
And works his sovereign will.

Blind unbelief is sure to err,
And scan his work in vain;
God is his own interpreter,
And he will make it plain.

William Cowper

January 17

St. Anthony, who is remembered today by Christians,
spent eighty years as a hermit, praying and worshipping
God.

"Jesus went out to a mountainside to pray, and spent the
night praying to God."

Luke 6

January 18

"Let us not be satisfied with just giving money.
Money is not enough, money can be got, but they need
your hearts to love them. So, spread love everywhere you
go: first of all in your own home. Give love to your children,
to your wife or husband, to a next door neighbor."

Mother Teresa of Calcutta

January 19

"Turn it as thou wilt, thou must give thyself to suffer what is appointed thee. But if we did that, God would bear us up at all times in all our sorrows and troubles, and God would lay His shoulder under our burdens, and help us to bear them. For if, with a cheerful courage, we submitted ourselves to God, no suffering would be unbearable."

J. Tauler

January 20

"There are no disappointments to those whose wills are buried in the will of God."

F.W. Faber

January 21

How hard it is to be a loyal soldier to Jesus Christ. I find Paul's words to the diffident, timid, young pastor Timothy, who is remembered today, most challenging:

"Take your part in suffering, as a loyal soldier of Christ Jesus. A soldier on active service wants to please his commanding officer and so does not get mixed up in the affairs of civilian life. An athlete who runs in a race cannot win the prize unless he obeys the rules."

2 Timothy 2:3–5

January 22

"For the love of God discipline your body and soul alike, keeping fit and healthy. If you should get ill, through circumstances beyond your control, bear it patiently and wait patiently upon God's mercy. That is all you need to do. It is true to say that patience in sickness and other forms of trouble pleases God much more than any splendid devotion that you might show in health."

The Cloud of Unknowing

January 23

Charles Kingsley, the champion of the underdog and the poor and author of such books as *The Water Babies* and *Westward Ho!*, died this day, 1875, and also wrote:

"I do not want to possess a faith,
I want a faith that possesses me."

January 24

"There is no greater valor nor no sterner fight than that for self–effacement, self-oblivion."

Meister Eckhart

January 25

Today Christians remember the apostle Paul. God's grace transformed this hate-filled persecutor of Christians into the apostle of Christ's love. Paul's most famous words from 1 Corinthians follow:

> "Love is patient,
> love is kind.
> It does not envy,
> it does not boast,
> it is not proud.
> It is not rude,
> it is not self-seeking
> it is not easily angered,
> it keeps no record of wrongs.
> Love does not delight in evil
> but rejoices with the truth.
> It always protects, always trusts,
> always hopes, always perseveres.
> ... And now these three remain:
> faith, hope and love.
> But the greatest of these is love."
>
> 1 Corinthians 13:4–7, 13

January 26

Interviewer: "If you had to live your life over again, what would you do differently?"

Billy Graham: "One of my great regrets is that I have not studied enough. I wish I had studied more and preached less."

January 27

The golden-tongued preacher of the fourth century, John Chrysostom, who is remembered on January 27, bequeathed us the following prayer: "Almighty God, who hast given us grace at this time with one accord to make our common supplications unto thee; and dost promise that when two or three are gathered together in thy Name, thou wilt grant their requests: fulfil now, O Lord, the desires and petitions of thy servants, as may be most expedient for them; granting us in this world knowledge of thy truth, and in the world to come life everlasting. Amen."

January 28

"Earth's crammed with heaven,
And every common bush afire with God;
But only he who sees takes off his shoes;
The rest sit round it and pluck blackberries."

Elizabeth Barrett Browning

January 29

"Men are qualified for civil liberties only to the extent that they are willing to put moral chains on their appetites."

Edmund Burke

January 30

On January 30, 1984, the English evangelist and Bible teacher David Watson wrote: "I am completely at peace – there is nothing I want more than to go to heaven. I know how good it is." A few weeks later he died of cancer.

January 31

Thomas Merton was born this day, 1915, in Prades, France. He wrote: "God, who is everywhere, never leaves us. Yet he seems sometimes to be present, sometimes absent. If we do not know him well, we do not realize that he may be more present to us when he is absent than when he is present."

FEBRUARY

February 1

May the strength of God pilot us.
May the power of God preserve us.
May the wisdom of God instruct us.
May the hand of God protect us.
May the way of God direct us,
and may the shield of God defend us,
now and evermore. Amen.

St. Patrick

February 2

"He that hath so many causes of joy, and so great, is very
much in love with sorrow and peevishness, who loses all
these pleasures, and chooses to sit down upon his little
handful of thorns. Enjoy the blessings of this day, if God
send them; and the evils of it bear patiently and sweetly:
for this day is only ours, we are dead to yesterday, and we
are not yet born to the morrow. But if we look abroad, and
bring into one day's thoughts the evil of many, certain and
uncertain, what will be and what will never be, our load
will be as intolerable as it is unreasonable."

Jeremy Taylor

February 3

"Love means to love that which is unlovable,
   or it is no virtue at all;
forgiving means to pardon the unpardonable,
   or it is no virtue at all;
faith means believing the unbelievable,
   or it is no virtue at all.
And to hope means hoping when things are hopeless,
   or it is no virtue at all."

G.K. Chesterton

February 4

"The Son of Man did not come to be served,
but to serve, and to give his life as a ransom
for many."

Matthew 20.28

February 5

"If thou hast Yesterday thy duty done,
And therby cleared firm footing for To–day
Whatever clouds make dark to–morrow's sun,
Thou shalt not miss thy solitary way."

J.W. Von Goethe

February 6

Jesus said, "I am the way the truth and the life. No one
comes to the Father except through me."

John 14:6

February 7

"Laughter is the nearest you can get to God."

Sarah Miles

February 8

God be in my head
     and in my understanding;
God be in my eyes
     and in my looking;
God be in my mouth
     and in my speaking;
God be in my heart
     and in my thinking;
God be in my end
     and at my departing.

Sarum Primer Prayer

February 9

"Do not look forward to the changes and chances
of this life in fear; rather look to them with
full hope that, as they arise God, whose
you are, will deliver you out of them.
He has kept you hitherto, – do you
but hold fast to his dear hand,
and he will lead you safely through
all things; and, when you cannot
stand, he will bear you in his arms.
Do not look forward to what may happen
tomorrow; the same everlasting Father
who cares for you today, will take care
of you tomorrow, and every day.
Either he will shield you from
suffering, or he will give you unfailing strength
to bear it. Be at peace then, and put aside all anxious
thoughts and imaginations."

Francis de Sales

February 10

"Do not be discouraged at your faults; bear
with yourself in correcting them, as you would with
your neighbor. Lay aside this ardor of mind, which
exhausts your body, and leads you to commit errors.
Accustom yourself gradually to carry prayer into all your
daily occupations. Speak, move, work, in peace, as if you
were in prayer, as indeed you ought to be."

Fenelon

February 11

Father of mercies, in thy word
What endless glory shines!
For ever be thy name adored
For these celestial lines.

Divine Instructor, gracious Lord,
O grant our fervent prayer;
Teach us to love thy sacred word,
And view the Saviour there.

A. Steele

February 12

"Beginning with Moses and the Prophets, Jesus explained to them what was said in all the Scriptures concerning himself. ... They asked each other, 'Were not our hearts burning within us while Jesus talked with us on the road and opened the Scriptures to us?'"

Luke 24:27, 32

February 13

Thou that hast given so much to me
Give one thing more, a grateful heart.
Not thankful when it pleaseth me,
As if thy blessings had spare days;
But such a heart, whose pulse may be thy praise.

George Herbert

February 14

Yard by yard, life is hard
Inch by inch, it's a cinch.

February 15

"It was not after we are reconciled by the blood of his Son that God began to love us, but before the foundation of the world."

John Calvin

February 16

Barbara Youderian became a widow when her husband was killed in 1956 by the Auca Indians. On learning the news of her husband's death she prayed, "Help me, Lord, to be both mummy and daddy."

February 17

"O Lord, whose way is perfect, help us, we pray thee, always to trust in thy goodness; that, walking with thee and following thee in simplicity, we may possess quiet and contented minds, and may cast all our care on thee, for thou carest for us; for the sake of Jesus Christ our Lord. Amen. "

Christina G. Rossetti

February 18

John Bunyan's *The Pilgrim's Progress* was first published on February 18, 1678. This extract is the Shepherd boy singing in the Valley of Humiliation:

> "He that is down needs fear no fall,
> He that is low no pride;
> He that is humble ever shall
> Have God to be his guide."

February 19
"In essentials, unity; in non-essentials, liberty;
in all things, charity."
Philipp Melanchthon

February 20
"If filled with the Spirit, you will be useful. You cannot help
being useful. Even if you were sick and unable to go out of
your room, or to converse, and saw nobody, you would be
ten times more useful than a hundred of those common
sorts of Christians who have no spirituality."
Charles G. Finney

February 21
"A little lie can travel half way around the world while
Truth is still lacing up her books."
Mark Twain

February 22

This day in 1327 the Inquisition made its response to Meister Eckhart's open declaration of faith in the grace of God. Eckhart, the father of the German mystics, wrote:

"God's greatest gifts to me are three. First, cessation of carnal desires and pleasures. Secondly, divine light enlightens me in everything I do. Thirdly, daily I grow and am renewed in God's grace."

February 23

Polycarp is remembered on February 23. As one of the early Christian martyrs the words he spoke before his martyrdom, when he was asked to retract his faith in Christ, continue to be an inspiration today:

"Eighty–six years have I served Jesus and he has done me no wrong. How can I blaspheme my king who saved me?"

February 24

"A moment's insight is sometimes worth a life's experience."

Oliver Wendell Holmes

February 25

"No one whose senses have been exercised to know good and evil can but grieve over the sight of zealous souls to be filled with the Holy Spirit while they are living in a state of moral carelessness and borderline sin. Whoever would be indwelt by the Spirit must judge his life for any hidden iniquities."

A.W. Tozer

February 26

"Our Father in heaven,
hallowed be your name,
your kingdom come,
your will be done
on earth as it is in heaven.
Give us today our daily bread.
Forgive us our debts,
as we forgive our debtors.
And lead us not into temptation,
but deliver us from the evil one."

Matthew 6:9–13

February 27

I asked God for strength that I might achieve;
I was made weak that I might learn humbly to obey.

I asked for help that I might do greater things;
I was given infirmity that I might do better things.

I asked for riches that I might be happy;
I was given poverty that I might be wise.

I asked for all things that I might enjoy life;
I was given life that I might enjoy all things.

I was given nothing that I asked for;
But everything that I had hoped for.

Despite myself, my prayers were answered;
I am among all men most richly blessed.

Anon.

February 28
"If you get simple beauty and nought else,
you get about the best thing God invents."
Robert Browning

February 29
"Men will not attend to what we say,
but examine into what we do; and will say,
'Do you first obey your own words, and then
exhort others.' This is the great battle, this is the
unanswerable demonstration, which is
made by our acts."
John Chrysostom

MARCH

March 1
"Give me my scallop shell of quiet,
My staff of faith to walk upon,
My script of joy, immortal diet,
My bottle of salvation,
My gown of glory, hope's true gage
And thus I'll take my pilgrimage."
Sir Walter Raleigh

March 2
"I am convinced the greatest act of love
we can ever perform for people is to tell them about
God's love for them in Christ."
Billy Graham

March 3
"Beauty is God's handwriting. Welcome it in every fair
face, every fair day, every fair flower."
Charles Kingsley

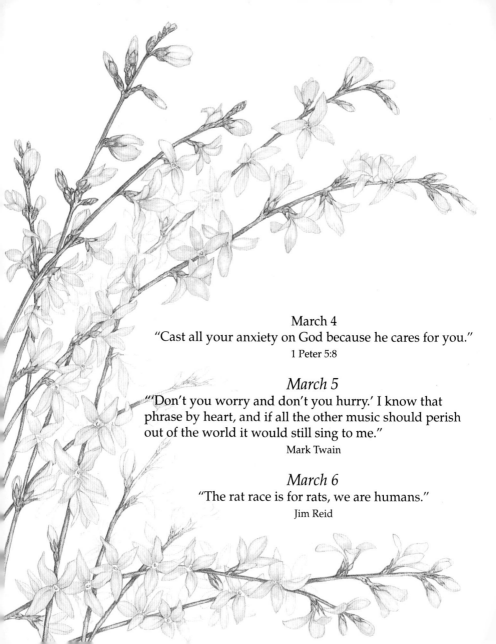

March 4
"Cast all your anxiety on God because he cares for you."
1 Peter 5:8

March 5
"'Don't you worry and don't you hurry.' I know that
phrase by heart, and if all the other music should perish
out of the world it would still sing to me."
Mark Twain

March 6
"The rat race is for rats, we are humans."
Jim Reid

March 7
"I would rather make mistakes in kindness
and compassion than work miracles in unkindness
and hardness."

Mother Teresa of Calcutta

March 8
On March 8, 1929, G.A. Studdert–Kennedy, known
as "Woodbine Willie," died of influenza, worn out in
God's service. He wrote:

"To give and give, and give again,
What God hath given thee;
To spend thyself nor count the cost,
To serve right gloriously
The God that gave all worlds that are,
And all that are to be."

March 9
"The spiritual leader influences others not by the power of
his own personality alone but by that personality irradiated
and interpenetrated and empowered by the Holy Spirit.
Because he permits the Holy Spirit undisputed control of
his life, the Spirit's power can flow through him to others
unhindered."

J. Oswald Sanders

March 10

Lord, our heavenly Father, almighty and everlasting God, who hast safely brought us to the beginning of this day: defend us in the same with thy mighty power; and grant that this day we fall into no sin, neither run into any kind of danger; but that all our doings may be ordered by thy governance, to do always that which is righteous in thy sight; through Jesus Christ our Lord. Amen.

The Book of Common Prayer

March 11

"Wisdom is oftentimes nearer when we stoop
than when we soar."

William Wordsworth

March 12

"As a deer longs for a stream of cool water,
so I long for you, O God.
I thirst for you, the living God;
when can I go and worship in your presence?

Why am I so sad?
why am I so troubled?
I will put my hope in God,
and once again I will praise him,
my savior and my God."

Psalm 42:1,2,11

March 13

"The Lord is my pace-setter, I shall not rush;
    he makes me stop and rest for quiet intervals,
    he provides me with images of stillness,
    which restore my serenity.
He leads me in the way of efficiency,
    through calmness of mind;
    and his guidance is peace.
Even though I have a great many things to accomplish
      each day
I will not fret, for his presence is here.
His timelessness, his all-important will keep me in balance.
He prepares refreshment and renewal
    in the midst of activity,
    by anointing my mind with his oils of tranquility;
    my cup of joyous energy overflows.
Surely harmony and effectiveness shall be
    the fruits of my hours
    and I will walk in the pace of my Lord,
    and dwell in his house for ever."

Toki Miyashina's version of Psalm 23

March 14

"Bread for myself is a material matter:
bread for other people is a spiritual matter."

Nikolai Berdyaev

March 15

For the beauty of the earth,
For the splendor of the skies,
For the love which from our birth
Over and around us lies,
Father, unto Thee we raise
This our sacrifice of praise.

For the joy of human love,
Brother, sister, parent, child,
Friends on earth, and friends above,
For all gentle thoughts and mild,
Father unto Thee we raise
This our sacrifice of praise.

F.S. Pierpoint

March 16

"When the church is prostrated in the dust before God,
and is in the depth of agony in prayer, the blessing does
them good. While at the same time, if they had received
the blessing without this deep prostration of soul, it would
have puffed them up with pride. But as it is, it increases
their holiness, their love, their humility."

Charles G. Finney

March 17

Today Irish people all around the world remember
their patron saint St. Patrick. One of his most famous
prayers follows:

"Christ be with me, Christ be within me,
Christ behind me, Christ before me,
Christ beside me, Christ to win me,
Christ to comfort me, and restore me,
Christ beneath me, Christ above me,
Christ in quiet, Christ in danger,
Christ in hearts of all that love me,
Christ in mouth of friend and stranger. Amen."

March 18

"I can do all things through Christ who strengthens me."
St. Paul in Philippians 4:13

March 19

When things get tough it helps to think of Christ by your
side. David Livingstone, the great explorer of Southern
Africa who was born this day, 1813, often said that the key
to his life was the verse, "I am with you always, to the very
end of the age."

March 20

One of the greatest promises in the Bible comes
from the letter to the Hebrews. "God has said, 'I will never
leave you; I will never abandon you.'"
Hebrews 13:5

March 21

Thomas Cranmer, writer of so much of the traditional
Anglican liturgy, was burned at the stake this day, 1556.
Grant to us, Lord, we beseech thee, the spirit to think and
do always such things as be rightful; that we, who cannot
do any thing that is good without thee, may by thee be
enabled to live according to thy will; through Jesus Christ
our Lord, Amen.

Collect for the Ninth Sunday After Trinity, from *The Book of Common Prayer*

March 22

Jonathan Edwards died this day, 1758, as a result of a
smallpox injection. One of his well-known sayings was,
"Grace is but glory begun, and glory is but grace
perfected."

March 23

In the hour of my distress,
When temptations me oppress,
And when I my sins confess;
Sweet Spirit comfort me!

When I lie within my bed,
Sick in heart, and sick in head,
And with doubts discomforted,
Sweet Spirit comfort me!

When the house doth sigh and weep,
And the world is drown'd in sleep,
Yet mine eyes the watch do keep;
Sweet Spirit comfort me!

When (God knows) I'm tossed about,
Either with despair, or doubt;
Yet before the glass be out,
Sweet Spirit comfort me!

When the judgment is reveal'd,
And that open'd which was seal'd,
When to Thee I have appeal'd;
Sweet Spirit comfort me!

Robert Herrick

March 24

Earth's crammed with heaven
and every common bush
afire with God.
And only he who sees
takes off his shoes.
The rest sit around
and pluck blackberries.

Elizabeth Barrett Browning

March 25

The Feast of the Annunciation of Mary is today and
we recall the humble song of praise:

"My soul glorifies the Lord
and my spirit rejoices in God my Savior,
for he has been mindful
of the humble state of his servant.
From now on all generations will call me blessed,
for the Mighty One has done great things for me–
holy is his name.
His mercy extends to those who hear him,
from generation to generation."

Luke 1:46-50

March 26

When I survey the wondrous cross
  On which the Prince of Glory died,
My richest gain I count but loss,
  And pour contempt on all my pride.

Forbid it, Lord, that I should boast,
  Save in the cross of Christ my God:
All the vain things that charm me most,
  I sacrifice them to his blood.

See from his head, his hands, his feet,
  Sorrow and love flow mingled down:
Did e'r such love and sorrow meet,
  Or thorns compose so rich a crown?

Were the whole realm of nature mine,
  That were an offering far too small;
Love so amazing, so divine,
  Demands my soul, my life, my all!

Isaac Watts

March 27

As a teenager the hymnwriter Frances Ridley Havergal was
sitting in the study of a German minister when she noticed
a cross on the wall, underneath which were the words,
"I did this for thee; what hast thou done for me?"

March 28
Today in 1515 Teresa de Cepeda y Ahumada
was born in Avila.

"Our Lord asks but two things of us: Love for him and for
our neighbor: this is what we must strive to obtain. Be sure
that as you make progress in brotherly love you are
increasing in your love for God. In this most important
matter we should be most watchful in little things, and take
no notice of the great works we plan during prayer."

The Interior Castle

March 29
"Fear God, and keep his commandments; for this is the
whole duty of man. For God will bring every deed into
judgment, with every secret thing, whether good or evil."

Ecclesiastes 12:13,14

March 30
Almighty Father,
look with mercy on this your family
for which our Lord Jesus Christ
was content to be betrayed
and given up into the hands of wicked men
and to suffer death upon the cross;
who is alive and glorified
with you and the Holy Spirit,
one God, now and for ever. Amen.

Adapted from the prayer for Good Friday in *The Book of Common Prayer*.

March 31
George Whitefield was one of the greatest preachers
of all times, keeping 20,000 people and more spellbound.
"I am compelled to preach. Woe to me if I do not preach
the gospel!"

An extract from his *Journal*, dated March 31, 1739.

APRIL

April 1

"Very early on Sunday morning the women went to the tomb carrying the spices they had prepared. They found the stone rolled away from the entrance to the tomb, so they went in; but they did not find the body of the Lord Jesus. They stood there puzzled about this, when suddenly two men in bright shining clothes stood by them. Full of fear, the women bowed down to the ground, as the men said to them, 'Why are you looking among the dead for one who is alive? He is not here; he has been raised. Remember what he said to you while he was in Galilee: "The Son of Man must be handed over to sinful men, be crucified, and three days later rise to life."'"

Luke's account of the resurrection, from Luke chapter 24:1–7

April 2

Abraham Lincoln, the greatest of all American presidents, was elected for a second term on this day. Let's remember to pray for the president with his awesome responsibility.

"We here highly resolve that the dead shall not have died in vain, that this nation, under God, shall have a new birth of freedom; and that government of the people, by the people, and for the people, shall not perish from the earth."

From his address at the Dedication of the National Cemetery at Gettysburg.

April 3

Thanks be to thee,
our Lord Jesus Christ:
for all the benefits
which thou hast given us;
for all the pains and insults
which thou hast borne for us.
O most merciful redeemer,
friend and brother:
may we know thee more clearly,
love thee more dearly,
and follow thee more nearly,
day by day.

Richard of Chichester, who died this day, 1253,
has had his beautiful prayer set to music many times.

April 4

Americans of all races mourned the death of Martin Luther King when an assassin's bullet killed him in Memphis, Tennessee, on April 4, 1968. The burden of his message was that of St. Paul's:

> "You are all sons of God through faith in Jesus Christ, for all of you who were baptized into Christ have clothed yourselves with Christ. There is neither Jew nor Greek, slave nor free, male nor female, for you are all one in Christ Jesus."
> Galatians 3:26–28

April 5

Dietrich Bonhoeffer, the German Protestant pastor and theologian, was arrested on April 5, 1943, and subsequently executed by the Gestapo. His most famous statement sums up his life.

"When Christ calls a man he bids him come and die."

April 6

It is in this month that those of us lucky enough to have a garden start planning for summer. I love these words by the seventeenth century writer Francis Bacon:

"God Almighty first planted a garden. And indeed it is one of the purest human pleasures. It is the greatest refreshment to the spirits of man; without which, buildings and palaces are but gross handyworks."

April 7

William Wordsworth was born today in 1770 at Cockermouth, Cumberland, England. He captures the spirit of April in his *Ode to a Daffodil*.

> "I wandered lonely as a cloud
> That floats on high o'er vales and hills,
> When all at once I saw a crowd,
> A host, of golden daffodils;
> Beside the lake, beneath the trees,
> Fluttering and dancing in the breeze...."

April 8

> "Keep in God's way; keep pace with every hour;
> Hurt none; do all the good that's in your power.
> Hours can't look back at all; they'll stay for none;
> Tread sure, keep up with them, and all's your own."

Francis Pastorius of Pennsylvania, a seventeenth century writer.

April 9

Gerard Manley Hopkins was a Jesuit priest of the last century whose desire to serve and worship God kept breaking forth in the most beautiful poetry.

"Nothing is so beautiful as Spring –
When weeds, in wheels, shoot long and lovely and lush;
Thrush's eggs look little low heavens, and thrush
Through the echoing timber does so rinse and wring
The ear, it strikes like lightnings to hear him sing;
The glassy peartree leaves and blooms, they brush
The descending blue; that blue is all in a rush
With richness; the racing lambs too have fair their fling."

April 10

Be encouraged in your fight against evil by remembering William Booth, born today in Nottingham, England in 1829, and who, in the Salvation Army, founded one of the world's finest organizations. Booth's motto was, "Go for souls, and go for the worst."

April 11

"Jesus said to Martha, 'I am the resurrection and the life. He who believes in me will live, even though he dies; and whoever lives and believes in me will never die.'"

John 11:25,26

April 12

In Russia, April 12 is celebrated as "Cosmonauts' Day" in memory of Yuri Gagarin's first space flight on April 12, 1961.

"Where shall I go from your Spirit?
Where can I flee from your presence?
If I go up to the heavens, you are there;
if I make my bed in the depths, you are there.
If I rise on the wings of the dawn,
if I settle on the far side of the sea,
even there your hand will guide me,
your right hand will hold me fast."

Psalm 139:7–10

April 13

"Kindness is a language which the blind can see and the deaf can hear."

Author unknown

April 14

"A good and wholesome thing is a little harmless fun in this world; it tones a body up and keeps him human and prevents him from souring."

Mark Twain

April 15

What a tragedy it was when the Titanic liner was lost on this day in 1912. Let's always keep the words of James in the New Testament in mind:

"Now listen to me, you that say, 'Today or tomorrow we will travel to a certain city, where we will stay a year and go into business and make a lot of money.' You don't even know what your life tomorrow will be! You are like a puff of smoke, which appears for a moment and then disappears. What you should say is this: 'If the Lord is willing, we will live and do this or that.'"

April 16

"Do not forget prayer. Every time you pray, if your prayer is sincere, there will be new feeling and new meaning in it, which will give you fresh courage."

Fyodor Dostoyevski

April 17

"When a train goes through a tunnel and it gets dark, you don't throw away your ticket and jump off. You sit still and trust the engineer."

Corrie ten Boom

April 18
Jeanne-Marie Bouvier de La Motte, better known
to us as Madame Guyon, was born this day in 1648.

"'Tis thine to number out our days;
'Tis ours to give them to thy praire."

April 19
"All God's life opens into the individual particular,
and here and now, or nowhere, is reality. The present
hour is the decisive hour and every day is doomsday."
Ralph Waldo Emerson

April 20

"Spring bursts today,
For Christ is risen and all the earth's at play."

Christina G. Rossetti

April 21

Anselm, Archbishop of Canterbury, was buried in
Canterbury Cathedral after he died this day in 1109.
Here is one of his most memorable prayers.

"O Lord our God,
grant us grace to desire thee with our whole heart,
that so desiring, we may seek and find thee;
and so finding thee we may love thee;
and loving thee we may hate those sins
from which thou hast redeemed us;
for the sake of Jesus Christ.
Amen. "

April 22

Yehudi Menuhin, the child prodigy on the violin,
was born today in 1916 in New York. Let's thank God
for the gift of music.

"Praise the Lord...
Praise him with the sounding of the trumpet,
praise him with the harp and lyre,
praise him with tambourine and dancing,
praise him with the strings and flute,
praise him with the clash of cymbals.
Let everything that has breath praise the Lord."

Psalm 150

April 23

"We are told in the Psalms, 'Sing to the Lord a new song.'
You may reply, 'I do sing to the Lord.'
Yes, of course you sing and I can hear you. But make sure
that your life sings the same tune as your mouth.
Sing with your voices.
Sing with your hearts.
Sing with your lips.
Sing with your lives.
Be yourselves what the words are about! If you live good
lives, you yourselves are the songs of new life."

St. Augustine

April 24

The United States Library of Congress, the largest
library in the world, was founded today in 1800.

"The fear of the Lord is the beginning of knowledge."

Proverbs 1:7

April 25

Today is the day in the Christian Year when we especially
remember Mark, the Gospel writer. He says that his gospel
is about "Jesus Christ, the Son of God" (1.1) who came
"to give his life as a ransom for many" (10:45), which sums
up the central fact and truth of the Christian gospel.

April 26

Be still, sad heart! and cease repining;
Behind the clouds the sun is shining;
Thy fate is the common fate of all,
Into each life some rain must fall.

Henry Wadsworth Longfellow

April 27

"There are only two duties required of us – the love
of God and the love of our neighbor, and the surest
sign of discovering whether we observe these duties
is the love of our neighbor."

Teresa of Avila

April 28

My God, my God, let me for once look on thee
As though nought else existed, me alone!
And as creation crumbles, my soul's spark
Expands until I can say – Even for myself
I need thee and I feel thee and I love thee.

Robert Browning

April 29

William Wilberforce, who died this day 1833, spent his parliamentary life crusading against the slave trade.

"Being aware of the absolute importance and arduous nature of the service in which he is engaged, the true Christian sets about his task with vigour and diligence. He is prepared to meet difficulties and is not discouraged when they occur."

April 30

My God! how wonderful thou art,
Thy Majesty how bright!
How beautiful thy mercy-seat,
In depths of burning light!

O how I fear thee, living God!
With deepest, tenderest fears;
And worship thee with trembling hope,
And penitential tears.

Yet may I love thee, too, O Lord,
Almighty as thou art;
For thou hast stooped to ask of me
The love of my poor heart.

Father of Jesus, love's Reward!
What rapture will it be,
Prostrate before thy thone to lie,
And gaze, and gaze on thee!

F.W. Faber

MAY

May 1
St. Philip and St. James's day

O Almighty God, whom truly to know is everlasting life:
Grant us perfectly to know thy Son Jesus Christ to be the
way, the truth, and the life; that, following the steps of thy
holy Apostles, Saint Philip and Saint James, we may
steadfastly walk in the way that leadeth to eternal life;
through the same thy Son Jesus Christ our Lord. Amen.

Collect for St. Philip and St. James's Day, from *The Book of Common Prayer*

May 2

"Lord, make me like crystal,
that your light may shine through me."

Katherine Mansfield

May 3

In Shakespeare's play King Henry VIII, the dying
Cardinal Wolsey charged Cromwell:

"Cromwell, I charge thee, fling away ambition:
by that sin fell the angels. How can man, then, the image
of his Maker, hope to gain by't?"

William Shakespeare

May 4

Jesus said: "What good will it be for a man if he gains the whole world, yet forfeits his own soul? Or what can a man give in exchange for his soul?"

Matthew 16:26

May 5

Round the Lord in glory seated,
Cherubim and seraphim
Filled his temple, and repeated
Each to each the alternate hymn,
"Lord, thy glory fills the heaven,
Earth is with its fulness stored;
Unto thee be glory given,
Holy, holy, holy Lord!"

R. Mant

May 6

O Lord God, when thou givest to thy servants to endeavor with any great matter, grant us also to know that it is not the beginning, but the continuing of the same to the end, until it be thoroughly finished, which yieldeth the true glory; through him who for the finishing of thy work laid down his life, our Redeemer, Jesus Christ. Amen.

Sir Francis Drake

May 7

"Let me offer you in sacrifice the service of
my thoughts and tongue. But first give me what
I may offer you."

St. Augustine

May 8

"Make us worthy, Lord, to serve our fellow men
throughout the world who die in poverty and hunger."

Mother Teresa of Calcutta

May 9

The leader of the German Moravian movement, Count
Zinzendorf, died this day, 1760. His motto was, "I have one
passion, it is Christ, Christ alone."

May 10

In 1882, D.L. Moody briefly revisited England and heard a preacher say: "The world has yet to see what God will do with a man fully consecrated to him." Moody resolved to be that man. The following prayer of his reflects this:

"Use me then, my Saviour, for whatever purpose, and in whatever way, you may require. Here is my poor heart, an empty vessel; fill it with your grace. Here is my sinful and troubled soul; quicken it and refresh it with your love."

May 11

"To understand God's thoughts we must study statistics, for these are the measure of his purpose."

Florence Nightingale, who is generally credited with founding modern nursing

May 12

"The vocation of every man and woman is to serve other people."

Leo Tolstoy

May 13

"To take up the cross of Christ is no great action done once for all; it consists in the continual practise of small duties which are distasteful to us."

John H. Newman

May 14

There is a book, who runs may read,
Which heavenly truth imparts;
And all the lore its scholars need –
Pure eyes and Christian hearts.

The works of God above, below,
Within us and around,
Are pages in that book, to show
How God himself is found.

The glorious sky, embracing all,
Is like the Maker's love,
Wherewith encompassed, great and small,
In peace and order move.

Thou who hast given me eyes to see
And love this sight so fair,
Give me a heart to find out thee,
And read thee everywhere.

John Keble

May 15

"The heavens declare the glory of God,
the skies proclaim the work of his hands."

Psalm 19:1

May 16

Ecclesiastes is always a mine of helpful reflection on how to live in
harmony with God and nature:

"Do not be quick with your mouth,
do not be hasty in your heart
to utter anything before God.
God is in heaven
and you are on earth,
so let your words be few."

Ecclesiastes 5:2

May 17

"Ten thousand difficulties do not make one doubt,"
John Cardinal Newman

May 18

"How many are your works, O Lord!
In wisdom you made them all;
the earth is full of your creatures."
Psalm 104:24

May 19

"I rejoice in following your statutes
as one rejoices in great riches.
I meditate on your precepts
and consider your ways.
I delight in your decrees;
I will not neglect your word."
Psalm 119:14-16

May 20

"Everything that is done in the world is done by hope."
Martin Luther

May 21

On May 21, 1521, Ignatius Loyola was struck by a French
cannonball that wounded his right leg and smashed his left
leg. Had this not happened we would have been the poorer
in not having this prayer of his.

"Teach us, good Lord, to serve thee as thou deservest;
to give and not to count the cost;
to fight and not to heed the wounds;
to toil and not to seek for rest;
to labor and not to ask for any reward
save that of knowing that we do thy will.
Amen."

May 22

"I am the true vine, and my Father is the gardener. He cuts off every branch in me that bears no fruit, while every branch that does bear fruit he prunes so that it will be even more fruitful. You are already clean because of the word I have spoken to you. Remain in me, and I will remain in you. No branch can bear fruit by itself; it must remain in the vine. Neither can you bear fruit unless you remain in me.

"I am the vine; you are the branches. If a man remains in me and I in him, he will bear much fruit; apart from me you can do nothing."

John 15:1–5

May 23

"Sow an act,
and you reap a habit.
Sow a habit,
and you reap a character.
Sow a character,
and you reap a destiny."

Charles Reade

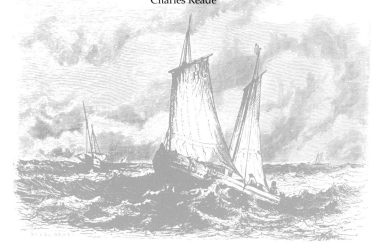

May 24

May 24, 1738, is the memorable day for all Methodists who recall that this was the day when John Wesley's heart was "strangely warmed" by God's grace. He traveled a quarter of a million miles on horseback and on foot preaching the gospel since he believed that "the world is my parish."

May 25

Take my life, and let it be
Consecrated, Lord, to Thee.
Take my moments and my days;
Let them flow in ceaseless praise . . .

Take my love; my Lord, I pour
At thy feet its treasure store.
Take myself, and I will be
Ever, only, all for Thee.

F.R. Havergal

May 26

"Let nothing disturb you;
let nothing dismay you;
all things pass:
God never changes.
Patience attains
all it strives for.
He who has God
finds he lacks nothing:
God alone suffices."

Teresa of Avila's bookmark

May 27

The great Bible teacher of the Reformation, John Calvin, died this day in 1564. Here is an extract from his *The Institutes of Christian Religion* on one of his favorite subjects: election.

"If we are searching for God's fatherly love and grace, we must look to Christ, in whom alone the Father is well pleased. If we are searching for salvation, life and immortality, we must turn to him again, since he alone is the fountain of life, the anchor of salvation and the heir of the kingdom. The purpose of election is no more than that, when we are adopted as sons by the heavenly Father, we will inherit salvation and eternal life through his favor."

May 28

"Take courage, and turn your troubles, which are without remedy, into material for spiritual progress. Often turn to our Lord, who is watching you, poor frail little being as you are, amid your labors and distractions. He sends you help, and blesses your affliction. This thought should enable you to bear your troubles patiently and gently, for love of him who only allows you to be tried for your own good. Raise your heart continually to God, seek his aid, and let the foundation stone of your consolation be your happiness in being his. All vexations and annoyances will be comparatively unimportant while you know that you have such a Friend, such a Stay, such a Refuge. May God be ever in your heart."

Francis de Sales

May 29

"In God alone is there faithfulness and faith
in the trust that we may hold to him, to his promise,
and to his guidance. To hold to God is to rely on
the fact that God is there for me, and to live
in this certainty.

Karl Barth

May 30

Jesus said, "I tell you, do not worry about your life, what
you will eat or drink; or about your body, what you will
wear. Is not life more important than food, and the body
more important than clothes? Look at the birds of the air;
they do not sow or reap or store away in barns, and yet
your heavenly Father feeds them. Are you not much more
valuable than they? Who of you by worrying can add a
single hour to his life? ... Therefore do not worry about
tomorrow, for tomorrow will worry about itself. Each day
has enough trouble of its own."

Matthew 6:25-27, 34

May 31

"Let God do with me what he will, anything he will;
whatever it be, it will be either heaven itself or some
beginning of it."

William Mountford

JUNE

June 1

Guide me, O thou great Jehovah!
Pilgrim through this barren land:
I am weak, but thou art mighty;
Hold me with thy powerful hand;
Bread of heaven,
Feed me till I want no more.

When I tread the verge of Jordan,
Bid my anxious fears subside;
Death of death, and hell's destruction,
Land me safe on Canaan's side;
Songs of praises
I will ever give to thee.

W. Williams and P. Williams

June 2

Jesus said,
"Blessed are the peacemakers,
for they will be called sons of God."

Matthew 5:9

June 3

"Have you ever thought seriously of the meaning of that blessing given to the peacemakers? People are always expecting to get peace in heaven; but you know whatever peace they get there will be ready-made. Whatever making of peace they can be blest for, must be on the earth here: not the taking of arms against, but the building of nests amidst, its 'sea of troubles' (like the halcyons). Difficult enough, you think? Perhaps so, but I do not see that any of us try. We complain of the want of many things– we want votes, we want liberty, we want amusement, we want money. Which of us feels or knows that he wants peace?"

J. Ruskin

June 4

"As soon as we are with God in faith and in love, we are in prayer."

Fenelon

June 5

Brother Lawrence experienced the presence of God, in his humble work in the kitchen of a monastery.

"Having found in many books different methods of going to God, and divers practices of the spiritual life, I thought this would serve rather to puzzle me, than facilitate what I sought after, which was nothing but how to become wholly God's. I began to live as though there was none but he and I in the world. I worshipped him as often as I could, keeping my mind in his holy presence."

June 6

"One grain of time's inestimable sand is worth a golden mountain: let us not lose it."

Roger Williams, the seventeenth century founder of Providence, in New England.

June 7

"Dinur, the Auschwitz survivor, is right — Eichmann is in us, each of us. But until we face the truth, dreadful as it may be, cheap grace and lukewarm faith – the hallmarks of ungrateful hearts – will continue to abound in a crippled church."

Charles Colson

June 8

O thou, who art the light of the minds that know thee, the life of the souls that love thee, and the strength of the wills that serve thee, help us so to know thee that we may truly love thee, so to love thee that we may fully serve thee, whom to serve is perfect freedom; through Jesus Christ our Lord. Amen.

Eighth Century prayer from the Gelasian Sacramentary.

June 9

O Lord, give us, we beseech thee, in the name of Jesus Christ thy Son, our Lord, that love which can never cease, that will kindle our lamps but not extinguish them, that they may burn in us and enlighten others. Amen.

Columba of Iona (one of the Western Isles of Scotland), who died in 597, is remembered on June 9 each year.

June 10

The Billy Graham Crusades have used this hymn at
the end of their meetings, throughout the world.

Just as I am, without one plea,
But that thy blood was shed for me,
And that thou bidd'st me come to thee,
O Lamb of God, I come!

Just as I am, though tossed about
With many a conflict, may a doubt,
Fighting and fears, within, without,
O Lamb of God, I come!

Just as I am, poor, wretched, blind;
Sight, riches, healing of the mind,
Yea, all I need, in thee, to find,
O Lamb of God, I come!

Just as I am, thou wilt receive,
Wilt welcome, pardon, cleanse, relieve;
Because thy promise I believe,
O Lamb of God, I come!

Just as I am, of that free love
The breadth, length, depth, and height to prove,
Here for a season, then above,
O Lamb of God, I come!

C. Elliot

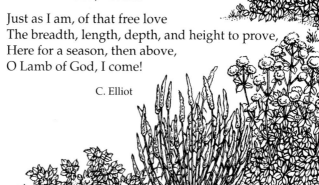

June 11

"First keep yourself in peace, and then you will
be able to pacify others. A peaceable man does
more good than a learned one. "

Thomas à Kempis

June 12

St. Augustine wrote these words as he reflected on how God
had drawn him to himself when he cared nothing for God.

"Late have I loved you, O Beauty so ancient and so
new; late have I loved you! For behold you were within
me, and I outside; and I sought you outside and in my
unloveliness fell upon those things that you have
made. You were with me and I was not with you. I was
kept from you by those things, yet had they not been in
you, they would not have been at all. You called and
cried to me and broke open my deafness; you sent your
shafts of light to shine on me and chase away my
blindness; you breathed your fragrant breath on me,
and I took a breath and now pant for you; I tasted you,
and now I hunger and thirst for you; you touched me
and I have burned for your peace."

June 13

"The essence of lying is in deception, not in words; a lie
may be told in silence, by equivocation, by the accent on a
syllable, by a glance of the eye attaching a peculiar
significance to a sentence; and all these kinds of lies are
worse and baser by many degrees than a lie plainly
worded; so that no form of blinded conscience is so far
sunk that which comforts itself for having deceived
because the deception was by gesture or silence, instead of
utterance."

J. Ruskin

June 14

"God wishes us to use the world and the blessings around us for our good but if we allow these things to draw us aside and to allure and stupefy us we will suffer great spiritual loss."

Sadhu Sundar Singh

June 15

The following verse brought the profligate Augustine to faith in Jesus Christ.

"Clothe yourselves with the Lord Jesus Christ, and do not think about how to gratify the desires of the sinful nature."

Romans 13:14

June 16

Jesus Christ said, "If the Son sets you free, you will be free indeed."

John 8:36

June 17

The memorial for Martin Luther King, Jr., reads as follows:

"Rev. Martin Luther King, Jr.
1929–1968
'Free at last, free at last,
Thank God A'mighty I'm free
at last!'"

June 18

Abbe Michel Quoist, born this day in Le Havre, in 1918, wrote, "The road to Jericho today, the road to the Good Samaritan, runs through every under-developed country."

June 19

England's most famous Baptist preacher, Charles Spurgeon, born this day, 1834, once said, "The Lord gets his best soldiers out of the highlands of affliction."

June 20

"He hath great tranquillity of heart who setteth nothing by praisings or blamings.

He whose conscience is clean, he will soon be content and pleased.

Thou art not the holier though thou be praised nor the more vile though thou be blamed or dispraised.

What thou art, that thou art; that God knoweth thee to be and thou canst be said to be no greater.

If thou take heed what thou art within thou shalt not care what men say of thee: man looketh on the face and God on the heart; many considereth the deeds and God praiseth the thoughts."

Thomas à Kempis

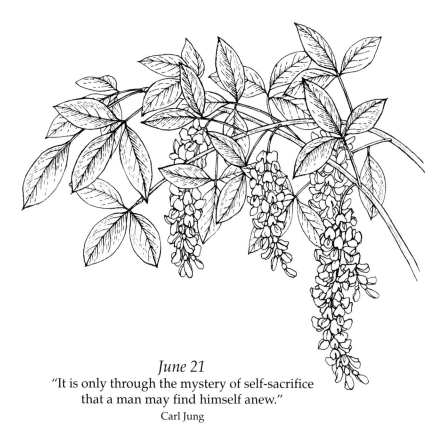

June 21
"It is only through the mystery of self-sacrifice
that a man may find himself anew."
Carl Jung

June 22
"The religion of Jesus has not just two letters DO,
but two more DONE."
Michael Green

June 23
"The Christian ideal has not been tried and found wanting,
it has been found difficult and left untried. "

G.K. Chesterton

June 24
The Feast Day of the Nativity of John the Baptist is
celebrated today with this reading from St. Luke's Gospel.

"When it was time for Elizabeth to have her baby,
she gave birth to a son. Her neighbors and relatives
heard that the Lord had shown her great mercy, and
they shared her joy. ...His father Zechariah asked for
a writing tablet, and to everyone's astonishment he
wrote, 'His name is John.'"

Luke 1:57,58, 63

June 25
John Calvin's motto was,
"My heart I give you, Lord,
eagerly and entirely."

June 26
"If any one would tell you the shortest, surest way to all
happiness and all perfection, he must tell you to make it a
rule to yourself to thank and praise God for everything that
happens to you. For it is certain that whatever calamity
happens to you, if you think and praise God for it, you turn
it into a blessing. Could you, therefore, work miracles, you
could not do more for yourself than by this thankful spirit;
for it heals with a word speaking, and turns all that it
touches into happiness."

William Law

June 27

Helen Keller was born on June 27, 1880, a normal
healthy baby, but was left deaf and totally blind
after an illness before she was two years old.
The story of her struggle against unequal odds, with
the help of her teacher and companion, Anne
Sullivan, has been translated into fifty languages.

"I believe that God is in me as the sun is in the color and
fragrance of a flower – the light in my darkness, the Voice
in my silence."

June 28

"Anxiety does not empty tomorrow of its sorrow –
only today of its strength."

C.H. Spurgeon

June 29

The traditional Bible reading for today, St. Peter's day,
comes from Matthew's Gospel, chapter 16, verses 15-18.

"'Who do you say I am?' Jesus asked his disciples.
Simon Peter answered, 'You are the Christ, the Son of the
living God.' Jesus replied, 'Blessed are you, Simon son of
Jonah, for this was not revealed to you by man, but by my
Father in heaven. And I tell you that you are Peter, and on
this rock I will build my church, and the gates of Hades
will not overcome it.'"

June 30

"The time for spiritual revival is now. We must not
delay. We do not know – any of us – how much time
we have left on this earth. Death may cut our lives
short. Christ could come again at any time."

Billy Graham

JULY

July 1

"O God, we thank you for this earth, our home; for the wide sky and the blessed sun, for the salt sea and the running water, for the everlasting hills and the never-resting winds, for trees and the common grass underfoot. We thank you for our senses by which we hear the songs of birds, O God our creator, who lives and reigns for ever and ever."

Walter Rauschenbusch

July 2

Sometimes God uses extraordinary circumstances to bring us to our senses. Martin Luther became a monk after he vowed, "St. Anne, I will become a monk!", as he feared for his life in the middle of a terrific thunderstorm.

July 3

"…those who are led by the Spirit of God
are sons of God."

Romans 8.14

July 4

In the left hand of the Statue of Liberty is a book of law on which is printed the date the United States declared its independence, July 4, 1776.

"Righteousness exalts a nation,
but sin is a disgrace to any people."

Proverbs 14:34

July 5
God's love is like the River Amazon flowing down to water
one daisy.

July 6
"To my God a heart of flame;
To my fellow man a heart of love;
To myself a heart of steel."

St. Augustine

July 7
"Love God.
Thrust down pride.
Forgive gladly.
Be sober of meat and drink.
Use honest company.
Reverence thine elders.
Trust in God's mercy.
Be always well occupied.
Lose no time.
Falling down, despair not.
Ever take a fresh, new, good purpose.
Persevere constantly.
Wash clean.
Be no sluggard.
Awake quickly.
Enrich thee with virtue.
Learn diligently.
Teach that thou has learned, lovingly."

John Colet's catechism for children

July 8

"If you confess with your mouth, 'Jesus is Lord,' and believe in your heart that God raised him from the dead, you will be saved."

Romans 10:10

July 9

"The Bible without the Holy Spirit is a sun-dial by moonlight."

D.L. Moody

July 10

On July 10, 1888, Toyohiko Kagawa was born in the Japanese port of Kobe. He spent his life determined to follow Christ's example and in the slums of Kobe, where people lived in appalling conditions he said, "If Christ were here, he would help them, and so must I."

July 11

Bernard of Clairvaux, who died this day, 1153, wrote, "All things are possible to one who believes."

July 12

"The one who comes into God's presence to pray must get rid of all boasting and self-opinionated ideas. Self-confidence must be thrown aside and God be given all the glory. Pride always means turning away from God. The holier the servant of God, the lower he will bow down in the presence of the Lord."

John Calvin, *Institutes of Christian Religion*

July 13

On July 13, 1960, C.S. Lewis' wife died of the cancer he knew she had before he married her. In his book *A Grief Observed* he writes of this traumatic event:

"Passionate grief does not link us with the dead, but cuts us off from them."

July 14

"I believe that the Bible is the best gift that God has ever given to man. All the good from the Savior of the world is communicated to us through this book.
I have been driven many times to my knees by the overwhelming conviction that I had nowhere else to go. "

Abraham Lincoln

July 15

"I am a great enemy to flies; when I have a good book, they flock upon it and parade up and down it, and soil it. 'Tis just the same with the devil. When our hearts are purest, he comes and soils them."

Martin Luther

July 16

"He gives strength to the weary
and increases the power of the weak.
Even youths grow tired and weary,
and young men stumble and fall;
but those who hope in the Lord
will renew their strength.
They will soar on wings like eagles;
they will run and not grow weary,
they will walk and not be faint."

The prophet Isaiah 40:29-31

July 17

Isaac Watts, born this day, 1674, sets our lives in their true perspective when he wrote:

> When I survey the wondrous cross
> On which the Prince of Glory died,
> My richest gain I count but loss,
> And pour contempt on all my pride.

July 18

"The best prayers are often more groans than words."

John Bunyan

July 19

"The Spirit helps us in our weakness. We do not know what we ought to pray for, but the Spirit himself intercedes for us with groans that words cannot express. And he who searches our hearts knows the mind of the Spirit, because the Spirit intercedes for the saints in accordance with God's will."

Romans 8:26-28

July 20

Love is that liquor sweet and most divine
Which my God sees as blood; but I as wine.

George Herbert

July 21

"I spent the evening praying incessantly for divine assistance and that I might not be self-dependent. What I passed through was remarkable, and there appeared to be nothing of any importance to me but holiness of heart and life, and the conversion of the heathen to God. I cared not where or how I lived, or what hardships I went through so that I could but gain souls to Christ."

Extracts taken from David Brainerd's diary, dated July 21, 1744

July 22

"When I consider how my light is spent
   Ere half my days in this dark world and wide,
   And that one talent is death to hide
   Lodged with me useless, though my soul more bent
To serve therewith my Maker, and present
   My true account, lest He returning chide,
   'Doth God exact day-labor, light denied?'
   I fondly ask. But Patience, to prevent
That murmur, soon replies, 'God doth not need
   Either man's work or his own gifts. Who best
   Bear his mild yoke, they serve him best. His state
Is kingly: thousands at his bidding speed,
   And post o'er land and ocean without rest;
   They also serve who only stand and wait.'"

"On His Blindness," John Milton

July 23

Jesus said, "I am the light of the world.
Whoever follows me will never walk in darkness,
but will have the light of life."

John 8:12

July 24

How sweet the name of Jesus sounds
In a believer's ear!
It soothes his sorrows, heals his wounds,
And drives away his fear.

It makes the wounded spirit whole
And calms the troubled breast;
'Tis manna to the hungry soul,
And to the weary rest.

Dear name! the rock on which I build,
My shield, and hiding-place,
My never-failing treasury, filled
With boundless stores of grace!

John Newton, born this day, 1725

July 25

St. James, apostle and martyr, is remembered today with
this extract from the Acts of the Apostles recording his
death. "King Herod had James, the brother of John, put to
death with the sword" (Acts 12:2). The other James, the
brother of Jesus, wrote, "Blessed is the man who perseveres
under trial, because when he has stood the test, he will
receive the crown of life that God has promised to those
who love him" (James 1:12).

July 26

Jim Elliot, who was killed by the Auca Indians, once said:

"I must not think it strange if God takes in youth those whom I would have kept on earth until they were older. God is peopling eternity, and I must not restrict him to old men and women."

July 27

No coward soul is mine,
No trembler in the world's storm-troubled sphere:
　　I see Heaven's glories shine,
And faith shines equal, arming me from fear.

O God within my breast,
Almighty, ever-present Deity!
　　Life – that in me has rest,
As I – undying Life – have power in thee!

Though earth and man were gone,
And suns and universes cease to be,
　　And thou wert left alone,
Every existence would exist in thee.

There is not room for Death,
Nor atom that his might could render void;
　　Thou– thou art Being and Breath,
And what thou art may never be destroyed.

Emily Bronte, her last lines before her death.

July 28

"I declare to you, brothers, that flesh and blood cannot inherit the kingdom of God, nor does the perishable inherit the imperishable. Listen, I tell you a mystery: We will not all sleep, but we will all be changed—in a flash, in the twinkling of an eye, at the last trumpet. For the trumpet will sound, the dead will be raised imperishable, and we will be changed."

1 Corinthians 15:50-52

July 29

Sigmund Freud's successor and survivor of a Nazi concentration camp, Viktor Frankl, believed that people curl up in a corner and die when they have no motive for living. He wrote:

"Any attempt to restore a man's inner strength in camp had first to succeed in showing him some future goal."

July 30

Dr. Aggrey of the Gold Coast, now Ghana, who died this day, 1927, said:

"God knew what he was doing when he made me black. On a piano you cannot play a good tune using only the white notes: you must use the black and white notes together. God wants to play tunes with both his white notes and his black ones."

July 31

"Death is the supreme festival on the road to freedom."

Dietrich Bonhoeffer

AUGUST

August 1

"For every leaf that rustles in the wind,
For spiring poplar, and for spreading oak,
For queenly birch, and lofty swaying elm;
For the great cedar's benedictory grace,
For earth's ten thousand fragrant incenses,
Sweet altar–gifts from leaf and fruit and flower.
For ripening summer and the harvesting,
We thank thee, Lord."

John Oxenham

August 2

"Sir Walter Scott expressed the wish, as he lay dying, that I should read to him, and when I asked him from what book, he said, 'Need you ask? There is but one.' I chose the fourteenth chapter of St. John's Gospel.

"'Jesus said, "Do not let your hearts be troubled. Trust in God; trust also in me. In my Father's house are many rooms; if it were not so, I would have told you. And I go and prepare a place for you, I will come back and take you to be with me that you also may be where I am. You know the way to the place where I am going."'

"Then Sir Walter Scott said, 'Well, this is a great comfort.'"

John Lockhart, Life of Sir Walter Scott

August 3

"True greatness consists in being great in litle things."

Dr. Johnson

August 4

"I have lived under the conviction that unearned suffering is redemptive. There are some who still find the cross a stumbling block, others consider it foolishness. But I am more convinced than ever, that it is the power of God to social and individual salvation."

Martin Luther King, Jr.

August 5

"I am nothing, I have nothing, I desire nothing but the love of Jesus in Jerusalem."

Walter Hilton

August 6

The Transfiguration of our Lord is remembered today.

"Jesus took with him Peter, James and John the brother of James, and led them up a high mountain by themselves. There he was transfigured before them. His face shone like the sun, and his clothes became white as the light. ...A cloud enveloped them, and a voice from the cloud said, 'This is my Son, whom I love; with him I am well pleased. Listen to him!'"

Matthew 17.1,2, 5

August 7

"Do not then forget Him, but think on Him often, adore Him continually, live and die with Him; this is the glorious employment of a Christian; in a word, this is our profession; if we do not know it we must learn it. I will endeavour to help you with my prayers."

Brother Lawrence

August 8

"O Lord God, when thou givest to thy servants to endeavour any great matter, grant us also to know that it is not the beginning, but the continuing of the same to the end, until it be thoroughly finished, which yieldeth the true glory; through him who for the finishing of thy work laid down his life, our Redeemer, Jesus Christ."

Sir Francis Drake

August 9

"What our Lord did was done with this intent, and this alone, that he might be with us and we with him."

Meister Eckhart

August 10

"Do small things as though they were great, because of the majesty of Jesus Christ who does them in us, and who lives in our lives. And do great things as though they were small and easy, because of his omnipotence."

Pascal

August 11

"It certainly takes grace to make a man into a saint. Anyone who doubts this does not know what a saint is—nor what a man is."

Pascal

August 12

"Nobody can fight properly and boldly for the faith if he clings to a fear of being stripped of earthly possessions."

St. Peter Damian

August 13

"A church that needs to be revived is a church that is living below the norm of the New Testament pattern. It is a tragic fact that the vast majority of Christians today are living a sub-normal Christian life. The church will never become normal until she sees revival."

James A. Stewart

August 14

"Let us also lay aside every encumbrance, and the sin which so easily entangles us, and let us run with endurance the race that is set before us, fixing our eyes on Jesus, the author and perfector of faith."

Hebrews 12:1,2

August 15

"At times almost all the wise and great of the earth have been pitted against the Bible, and only an obscure few for it. Yet it has stood."

R.A. Torrey

August 16

"Who shuts his hand has lost his gold
Who opens it hath it twice told."

George Herbert

August 17

"It is so hard to believe because it is so hard to obey."

Soren Kierkegaard

August 18

"I do not seek to understand that I may believe, but I believe that I may understand."

Anselm

August 19

"Like anybody else, I would like to live a long life. Longevity has its place. But I'm not concerned about that now. I just want to do God's will."

Spoken by Martin Luther King, Jr, the night before he was shot.

August 20

St. Bernard of Clairvaux is remembered today. A prayer verse of his follows:

O Jesus, ever with us stay;
Make all our moments calm and bright;
Chase the dark night of sin away;
Shed o'er the world thy holy light. Amen.

August 21

Francis de Sales, who was born this day, 1567,
was asked by a nun on his death bed to write down
the virtue he most desired. He wrote one word:
Humility.

August 22

"Do not measure yourself by others,
who may not be led as you are.
God chooses to enrich some souls with
brilliant gifts, but he has chosen you,
stripped of all, in the depths of
spiritual poverty."

From one of Madame Guyon's letters

August 23

"We cannot become saints merely by trying to run away from material things. To have a spiritual life is to have a life that is spiritual in all its wholeness – a life in which the actions of the body are holy because of the soul, and the soul is holy because of God dwelling and acting in it. When we live such a life, the actions of our body are directed to God by God himself and give him glory, and at the same time they help to sanctify the soul."

Thomas Merton

August 24

"Well-done is better than well-said."

Benjamin Franklin

August 25

"In all toil there is profit, but mere talk tends only to want"

Proverbs 14:23

August 26

"I saw three properties; that first is, that God made it. The second is, that God loveth it. The third is, that God keepeth it. But what beheld I therein? Verily the Maker, the Keeper, the Lover."

Julian of Norwich

August 27

"Courage faces fear and thereby masters it. Cowardice represses fear and is thereby mastered by it."

Martin Luther King, Jr.

August 28

"O Lord, who though thou wast rich, yet for our sakes didst become poor, and hast promised in thy gospel that whatsoever is done unto the least of thy brethren, thou wilt receive as done unto thee: give us grace, we humbly beseech thee, to be ever willing and ready to minister to the needs of our fellow creatures, to thy praise and glory who art God over all. Amen."

A prayer of St. Augustine of Hippo, who died this day, 430.

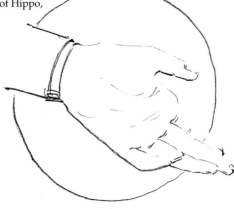

August 29

Charles Finney, born this day, 1792, in Warren, Connecticut, has left us many volumes about revival. His words are as challenging and relevant today as when they were first written.

"A revival may be expected whenever Christians are found willing to make the sacrifices necessary to carry it on. They must be willing to sacrifice their feelings, their business, their time, to help forward the work."

August 30

"Back to the Bible, or back to the jungle."

Evangelist Luis Palau

August 31

The famous German theologian, Karl Barth, was once asked to sum up what he believed. He replied, "Jesus loves me, this I know, for the Bible tells me so."

SEPTEMBER

September 1

Praised be you, my Lord, through our Sister Mother Earth, who sustains us, governs us, and who produces varied fruits with colored flowers and herbs.

Praised be you, my Lord, through Brother Wind and through the air, cloudy and serene, and every kind of weather.

Praised be you, my Lord, through Sister Moon and the stars in heaven: you formed them clear and precious and beautiful.

Praised be you, my Lord, through Brother Fire, through whom you light the night and he is beautiful and playful and robust and strong.

Praised be you, my Lord, with all your creatures, especially Sir Brother Sun, who is the day and through whom you give us light. And he is beautiful and radiant with great splendors and bears likeness of You, Most High One.

Francis of Assisi

September 2
"Make every effort to live in peace with all men and to be holy; without holiness no-one will see the Lord."
Hebrews 12:14

September 3
"What we weave in time we wear in eternity. The road to hell is paved with good intentions."
J.C. Ryle

September 4
"Christian perfection is loving God with all our heart, mind, soul, and strength. This implies, that no wrong frame of mind, nothing contrary to love, remains in the soul; and that all the thoughts, words and actions, are governed by pure love."
John Wesley

September 5

And can it be that I should gain
An interest in the Savior's blood!
Died he for me, who caused his pain?
Amazing love! how can it be
That thou, my God, shouldst die for me!

No condemnation now I dread;
Jesus, and all in him, is mine!
Alive in him, my living head,
And clothed in righteousness divine,
Bold I approach the eternal throne,
And claim the crown, through Christ, my own.

Charles Wesley

September 6

"The early Christian Church was not an organization merely, not a movement, but a walking incarnation of spiritual energy. And she accomplished within a few brief years such prodigies of moral conquest as to leave us wholly without an explanation—apart from God."

A.W. Tozer

September 7

"One must not always think so much about what one should do, but rather what one should be. Our works do not ennoble us; but we muust ennoble our works."

Meister Eckhart

September 8

"Do not boast about tomorrow,
for you do not know what a day may bring forth."

Proverbs 27:1

September 9

"Contemplation is nothing else but a secret,
peaceful, and loving infusion of God,
which, if admitted, will set the soul on fire
with the spirit of love."

St. John of the Cross

September 10
"There is medicine in the Bible for every sin-sick soul,
but every soul does not need the same medicine."

R.A. Torrey

September 11
"Watergate caused my world to crack around me
and sent me to prison. I lost the mainstay of my
existence – the awards, the six-figure income and
lifestyle to match, a position of power at the right
hand of the President of the United States.
But only when I lost them did I find a far
greater gain: knowing Christ."

Charles Colson

September 12
"Christianity has taught us to care.
Caring is the greatest thing, caring matters most."
Friedrich von Hugel

September 13
"Blessed are those who saw Christ in the flesh. But still
more blessed are we who see his image portrayed in
the Gospels, and hear his voice speaking from them."
St. Tikhon of Zadonsk

September 14
"Jesus said to his disciples, 'If anyone would come after
me, he must deny himself and take up his cross and
follow me. For whoever wants to save his life will lose it,
but whoever loses his life for me will find it.'"
Matthew 16:24,25

September 15
"My heaven is to please God and glorify him,
and to give all to him, and to be wholly devoted
to his glory; that is the heaven I long for."
David Brainerd

September 16

Amazing grace! How sweet the sound
    That saved a wretch like me.
I once was lost, but now am found,
    Was blind, but now I see.

'Twas grace that taught my heart to fear,
    And grace my fears relieved.
How precious did that grace appear
    That hour I first believed.

Through many dangers, toils and snares,
    I have already come;
'Tis grace has brought me safe thus far,
    And grace will lead me home.

When we've been there ten thousand years,
    Bright shining as the sun,
We've no less days to sing God's praise
    Than when we've first begun.

John Newton

September 17
Jesus said,
"Greater love has no one than this,
that he lay down his life for his friends."
John 15:13

September 18
"Let us make God the beginning and end of our
love, for he is the fountain from which all good
things flow and into him alone they flow back.
Let him therefore be the beginning of our love."
Richard Rolle

September 19

Here is an extract from a letter that Dr. Barnardo, who died today in 1905, wrote towards the end of his life.

"What a wonderful experience mine has been during these thirty-nine years! What inexhaustible supplies have been vouchsafed to the work in my hands. How amazing to mere unaided human reason have been the answers to prayer, even when faith has almost failed and our timidity has begotton distrust instead of love and hope! And God has not failed us once!"

September 20

"Only as men receive the love of God shed abroad on Calvary can they work together to solve the problems that plague the entire world."

Billy Graham's thoughts at the end of his crusade to Africa in 1960

September 21

On *St. Matthew's Day* we recall Jesus calling Matthew to be his disciple.

"Jesus saw a man named Matthew sitting at the tax collector's booth. 'Follow me,' he told him, and Matthew got up and followed him."

"While Jesus was having dinner at Matthew's house, many tax collectors and 'sinners' came and ate with him and his disciples. When the Pharisees saw this, they asked his disciples, 'Why does your teacher eat with tax collectors and "sinners"?'

"On hearing this, Jesus said, 'It is not the healthy who need a doctor, but the sick. But go and learn what this means: "I desire mercy, not sacrifice." For I have not come to call the righteous, but sinners.'"

Matthew 9:9-13

September 22
"Do all the good you can
By all the means you can
In all the ways you can
In all the places you can
To all the people you can
As long as ever you can."
John Wesley

September 23
"He who shall introduce into public affairs
the principle of primitive Christianity will change
the face of the world."
Benjamin Franklin

September 24

"My heart leaps when I behold
A rainbow in the sky:
So was it when my life began;
So it is now I am a man;
So be it when I shall grow old,
Oh let me die!
The Child is the father of the Man;
And I could wish my days to be
Bound each to each by natural piety."

William Wordsworth

September 25

"I charge you before the Lord Jesus Christ, who giveth life,
and more abundant life—I entreat you by all the actings of
faith, the exertions of hope, the flames of love you ever felt,
sink to greater depths of self-abasing repentance, and rise
to greater heights of Christ-exalting joy."

John Fletcher

September 26

"The only wisdom we can hope to acquire
is the wisdom of humility."

T.S. Eliot, born this day, 1888, in St. Louis

September 27

"Our heavenly Father never takes anything
from his children unless he means to give them
something better."

George Muller, the philanthropist from Kroppenstadt,
was born this day, 1805

September 28

"We cannot read the Bible without being impressed by its constant emphasis one the efficacy of prayer. 'The prayer of a righteous man is powerful and effective,' wrote James (5:16). We do not claim to understand the rationale of intercession. But somehow it enables us to enter the field of spiritual conflict, and to align ourselves with the good purposes of God, so that his power is released and the principalities of evil are bound."

John Stott

September 29

We remember today, Michaelmas Day, how Michael and his angels defeated the devil.

"And there was war in heaven. Michael and his angels fought against the dragon, and the dragon and his angels fought back. But he was not strong enough, and they lost their place in heaven. The great dragon was hurled down—that ancient serpent called the devil, or Satan, who leads the whole world astray. He was hurled to the earth, and his angels with him. "Then I heard a loud voice in heaven say: 'Now have come salvation and the power and the kingdom of our God, and the authority of his Christ.'"

Revelation 12:7-10

September 30

This is the day on which the fourth century Bible translator Jerome is remembered. Here is one of his prayers.

"O Lord, you have given us your word for a light to shine upon our path; grant us so to meditate on that word, and to follow its teaching, that we may find in it the light that shines more and more until the perfect day; through Jesus Christ our Lord, Amen."

OCTOBER

October 1

Season of mists and mellow fruitfulness,
Close bosom-friend of the maturing sun;
Conspiring with him how to load and bless
With fruit the vines that round the thatch-eves run;
To bend with apples the moss'd cottage trees,
And fill all fruit with ripeness to the core;
To swell the gourd, and plump the hazel shells
With a sweet kernel; to set budding more,
And still more, later flowers for the bees,
Until they think warm days will never cease,
For summer has o'er-brimmed their clammy cells.

John Keats, "To Autumn"

October 2

William Carey started a fund on October 2, 1792,
for the newly formed Baptist Missionary Society
and he and his fellow ministers raised £13. 2s. 6d.
for this! This was in response to being told,
"When God wills to convert the heathen world,
young man, he'll do it without consulting you
or me."

October 3

"Dear friends, let us love one another, for love comes from God. Everyone who loves has been born of God and knows God. Whoever does not love does not know God, because God is love. This is how God showed his love among us: He sent his one and only Son into the world that we might live through him. This is love: not that we loved God, but that he loved us and sent his Son as an atoning sacrifice for our sins. Dear friends, since God so loved us, we also ought to love one another. No one has ever seen God, but if we love one another, God lives in us and his love is made complete in us."

1 John 4:7–12

October 4

The following prayer is traditionally ascribed to St. Francis of Assisi. Today we remember St. Francis, who gave away all his rich possessions and fine clothing.

Eternal God, the Father of all mankind:
we commit to thee the needs of the whole world:
where there is hatred, give love;
where there is injury, pardon;
where there is distrust, faith;
where there is sorrow, hope;
where there is darkness, light;
through Jesus Christ our Lord.
Amen.

October 5

"A religion which does not make us kind
is not our Lord's religion."

"The Christlike Christian," by An Unknown Christian

October 6

The Bible translator William Tyndale was
martyred on October 6, 1536. When he was a young man
the Bible was still only translated in Latin. In an argument
with a scholar he said:

"If God spare my life, 'ere many years I will cause
a boy who drives the plough to know more of the
Scriptures than you do."

October 7

Henry Alford, born in London on October 7, 1810, left
us many devotional hymns and prayers. Here is one
of his prayers:

"O Lord, give us more charity, more self-denial, more
likeness to thee. Teach us to sacrifice our comforts to
others, and our likings for the sake of doing good.
Make us kindly in thought, gentle in word, generous in
deed.
Teach us that it is better to give than to receive; better to
forget ourselves than to put ourselves forward; better
to minister than to be ministered unto.
And unto thee, the God of love, be glory and praise for
ever."

October 8

"God opposes the proud
but gives grace to the humble."

Proverbs 3:34

October 9

At the age of twenty-nine, on October 9, 1747, David Brainerd died. This is the last entry he made in his diary before his death.

"I was a little better than speechless all day. I My God, I am speedily coming to thee! Hasten the day, O Lord, if it be thy blessed will. Oh, come, Lord Jesus, come quickly."

October 10

Blessed assurance, Jesus is mine;
O what a foretaste of glory divine!
Heir of salvation, purchase of God;
Born of his Spirit, washed in his blood.

This is my story, this is my song,
Praising my Savior all the day long.

Perfect submission, perfect delight,
Visions of rapture burst on my sight;
Angels descending, bring from above
Echoes of mercy, whispers of love.

Perfect submission, all is at rest,
I in my Savior am happy and blest;
Watching and waiting, looking above,
Filled with his goodness, lost in his love.

Frances Van Alstyne

October 11

"There are but these three classes of men: those
who have found God, and serve him; those that have
not yet found him, but seek him earnestly; those
who spend their lives neither seeking nor finding.
The first know where the true values lie, and they
are happy; the last are stupid and unhappy; the class
in the middle are unhappy, but they are rational."

Pascal

October 12

"All things are possible to him who believes,
yet more to him who hopes, more still to him
who loves, and most of all to him who practices
and perseveres in these three virtues."

Brother Lawrence

October 13

"Christ is not valued at all unless
he be valued above all."

Augustine of Hippo

October 14

"The Bible is the greatest traveler in the world. It
pentrates to every country, civilized and uncivilized.
It is seen in the royal palace and in the humble
cottage. It is the friend of emperors and beggars.
It is read by the light of the dim candle amid Arctic
snows. It is read under the glare of the equatorial sun.
It is read in city and country, amid the crowds and in
solitude. Wherever its message is received, it frees the
mind from bondage and fills the heart with gladness."

Dr A.T. Pierson

October 15

On October 15, 1932, Gladys Aylward, a little parlour maid, left Liverpool Street Station, London on her journey to China where she was certain God wanted her to work for him. She wrote in 1941:

"I have two planks for a bed, two stools, two cups and a basin. On my broken wall is a small card which says, 'God hath chosen the weak things – I can do all things through Christ who strengthens me.' It is true I have passed through fire."

October 16

Bishop Ridley and Bishop Latimer were both burned at the stake at Oxford on October 16, 1555. As the flames started Latimer said to Ridley, "Be of good comfort, Master Ridley: play the man: we shall this day light such a candle, by God's grace, in England, as I trust shall never be put out."

October 17

O happy day that fixed my choice
On you, my Savior and my God!
Well may this grateful heart rejoice
And tell of Christ's redeeming blood.

O happy day, O happy day,
When Jesus washed my sins away,
He taught me how to watch and pray,
And live rejoicing ev'ry day; (Hallelujah!)
O happy day, O happy day,
When Jesus washed my sins away.

Philip Doddridge

October 18

St. Luke's Day is remembered today with his record of one of Jesus' most loved parables.

"Then Jesus told them this parable:
'Suppose one of you has a hundred sheep and loses one of them. Does he not leave the ninety-nine in the open country and go after the lost sheep until he finds it? And when he finds it, he joyfully puts it on his shoulders and goes home. Then he calls his friends and neighbors together and says, "Rejoice with me; I have found my lost sheep." I tell you that in the same way there will be more rejoicing in heaven over one sinner who repents than over ninety-nine righteous persons who do not need to repent.'"

Luke 15:3-7

October 19

O God, who hast prepared for them that love thee such good things as pass man's understanding: Pour into our hearts such love toward thee, that we, loving thee above all things, may obtain thy promises, which exceed all that we can desire; through Jesus Christ our Lord. Amen.

Collect for the Sixth Sunday after Trinity, from
The Book of Common Prayer

October 20

"All the graces of a Christian
spring from the death of self."

Madame Guyon

October 21

"Christ's system of morals and religion as he left them to us is the best the world has seen or is likely to see."

Benjamin Franklin

October 22

"I am not what I ought to be: I am not what I wish to be: I am not what I hope to be: but by the grace of God I am what I am."

John Newton

October 23

"Dear friends, now we are children of God, and what we will be has not yet been made known. But we know that when Christ appears, we shall be like him, for we shall see him as he is. Everyone who has this hope in him purifies himself, just as he is pure."

1 John 3:2,3

October 24

"I know of nothing better than to keep my eye on my great sinfulness" was the reply the nineteeth-century American evangelist Asahel Nettleton gave in reply to the question, "How do you safeguard against spiritual pride?"

October 25

"We are the Bibles the world is reading;
We are the creeds the world is needing;
We are the sermons the world is heeding."

Billy Graham

October 26

The Lord God says,
"Do not fear, for I am with you;
Do not be dismayed, for I am your God.
I will strengthen you and help you;
I will uphold you with my righteous right hand."

The prophet Isaiah 41:10

October 27

"Therefore, I urge you, brothers, in view of God's mercy, to offer your bodies as living sacrifices, holy and pleasing to God – this is your spiritual act of worship. Do not conform any longer to the pattern of this world, but be transformed by the renewing of your mind."

Romans 12:1,2

October 28

On October 28, 1618, the day before he was beheaded,
Sir Walter Raleigh wrote:

> "Even such is time which takes in trust
> Our youth, our joys, and all we have
> And pays us but with age and dust:
> Who in the dark and silent grave
> When we have wandered all our ways
> Shuts up the story of our days.
> And from the earth and grave and dust
> The Lord shall raise me up I trust."

October 29

"God respects me when I work,
but he loves me when I sing."

Rabindranath Tagore

October 30
"To be 'whole' is to be spiritually, emotionally and physically healthy. Jesus lived in perfect wholeness."
Colin Urquhart

October 31
"The time has come for my departure. I have fought the good fight, I have finished the race, I have kept the faith. Now there is in store for me the crown of righteousness, which the Lord, the righteous Judge, will award to me on that day – and not only to me, but also to all who have longed for his appearing."
2 Timothy 4:6-8

NOVEMBER

November 1
All Saint's Day

"Mr Valiant-for-Truth said, 'I am going to my Father's; and though with great difficulty I have got hither, yet now I do not repent me of all the trouble I have been at to arrive where I am. ...My marks and scars I carry with me, to be a witness for me that I have fought his battles, who now will be my rewarder.' When the day that he must go hence was come, many accompanied him to the river-side; into which, as he went, he said, 'Death, where is thy sting?' And as he went deeper he said, 'Grave, where is thy victory?' So he passed over, and all the trumpets sounded for him on the other side."

John Bunyan, *The Pilgrim's Progress*

November 2

These words of Abraham Lincoln
are most appropriate for All Souls' Day:

"The Lord prefers
common-looking people.
That is the reason he makes
so many of them."

November 3

The "father of Sunday Schools," Robert Raikes, used his own newspaper, *The Gloucester Journal*, on November 3, 1783, to launch his appeal for money for his Sunday schools.

There is a remarkable incident recorded in Matthew 19:13-15 about Jesus' attitude towards children:

"Some people brought children to Jesus for him to place his hands on them and to pray for them, but the disciples scolded the people. Jesus said, 'Let the children come to me and do not stop them, because the Kingdom of Heaven belongs to such as these.' He placed his hands on them and then went away."

November 4

"We do the works, but God in us the doing of the works."

St. Augustine

November 5

"Now let us do something beautiful for God."

Mother Teresa of Calcutta, written in a letter to a friend.

November 6

Glory be to God for dappled things –
    For skies of couple-color as a brinded cow;
    For rose–moles all in stipple upon trout that swim;
Fresh-firecoal chestnut-falls; finches' wings;
    Landscape plotted and pieced – fold, fallow,
        and plough;
    And all trades, their gear and tackle and trim.

All things counter, original, spare, strange;
    Whatever is fickle, freckled (who knows how?)
    With swift, slow; sweet, sour; adazzle, dim;
He fathers-forth whose beauty is past change:
    Praise him

Gerard Manley Hopkins

November 7

Billy Graham, one of the modern "saints of God,"
born this day, 1918, has as his favorite Bible verse:

> "For God so loved the world that he gave his
> one and only Son, that whoever believes in him
> shall not perish but have eternal life."

John 3:16

November 8

It is a thing most wonderful
Almost too wonderful to be
That God's own Son should come from heaven
And die to save a child like me.

W.W. How

November 9
"See what you lack and not what you have,
for that is the quickest path to humility."
Cloud of Unknowing

November 10
O Jesus, I have promised
To serve Thee to the end;
Be Thou for ever near me,
My master and my friend;
I shall not fear the battle
If Thou art by my side,
Nor wander fromthe pathway
If Thou wilt be my guide.
J.E. Bode

November 11
On this day in 1855 Søren Kierkegaard died
in Copenhagen. He wrote, "If a man in truth wills the Good
then he must be willing to suffer for the Good."

November 12
"The man who is truly forgiven and knows it,
is a man who forgives."
Martyn Lloyd-Jones

November 13

John Bunyan, in *The Pilgrim's Progress*, tells how Pilgrim with his burden arrived at the cross, and looked by faith to the Savior, and his burden fell off and was buried in the grave. He then exclaimed:

"Blessed cross! Blest sepulchre! Blest rather be
The Man that there was put to shame for me."

November 14

Paul wrote these wonderful words in his letter
to the Galatians, chapter 2, verse 20.

"I have been crucified with Christ and I no longer live, but Christ lives in me. The life I live in the body, I live by faith in the Son of God, who loved me and gave himself for me."

November 15

"O for a closer walk with God,
A calm and heavenly frame,
A light to shine upon the road
That leads me to the Lamb."

From *the Olney hymns*, by William Cowper,
who was born on November 15, 1731

November 16

Defend, O Lord, this thy child with thy heavenly grace that he may continue thine for ever; and daily increase in thy Holy Spirit, more and more, until he comes unto thy everlasting kingdom. Amen.

Prayer from the Anglican Confirmation Service

November 17

"More things are wrought by prayer than this world
　　dreams of:
For what are men better than sheep or goats
If, knowing God, they lift not hands of prayer
Both for themselves and those who call them friend."

Alfred, Lord Tennyson

November 18

Two it takes to make a quarrel.
One can always end it.

November 19

Charles Dickens was once asked what he thought
was the best short story in the English language, and
he replied: "The Prodigal Son."

November 20

"But while the prodigal son was still a long way off,
his father saw him and was filled with compassion
for him; he ran to his son, threw his arms around
him and kissed him."

Luke 15:20

November 21

Interviewer: "How do you see yourself as having
　　changed in the years since your conversion?"
Charles Colson: "My priorities before were power, wealth,
　　fame; today I believe they are knowing and loving
　　God, my relationship with my family, which have
　　become much more meaningful to me, and my
　　desire to serve the Lord."

November 22

Jesus said, "Look at the birds of the air; they do not sow
or reap or store away in barns, and yet your heavenly
Father feeds them. Are you not much more valuable
than they? Who of you by worrying can add a single
hour to his life?

"And why do you worry about clothes? See how
the lilies of the field grow. They do not labor or spin.
Yet I tell you that not even Solomon in all his splendor
was dressed like one of these. If that is how God
clothes the grass of the field, which is here today
and tomorrow is thrown into the fire, will he not
much more clothe you, O you of little faith?"

Matthew 6:25-30

November 23

"Consider
The lilies of the field whose bloom is brief:
We are as they;
Like them we fade away,
As doth a leaf.

Consider
The sparrows of the air of small account;
Our God doth view
Whether they fall or mount,
He guards us too.

Consider
The lilies do neither spin nor toil,
Yet are most fair:
What profits all this care
And all this toil?

Consider
The birds that have no barn nor harvest-weeks;
God gives them food:
Much more our Father seeks
To do us good.

Christina G. Rossetti

November 24
John Knox died this day, 1572,
and his dying words were, "Live in Christ, live in Christ,
and the flesh need not fear death."

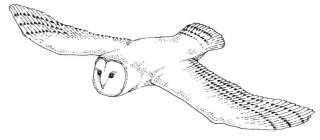

November 25

"When the Spirit came to Moses, the plagues came
upon Egypt, and he had power to destroy men's lives;
when the Spirit came upon Elijah, fire came down from
heaven; when the Spirit came upon Joshua, he moved
around the city of Jericho, and the whole city fell into his
hands. But when the Spirit came upon the Son of Man,
he gave his life, he healed the broken-hearted."

D.L. Moody

November 26

For feelings come and feelings go,
    And feelings are deceiving.
My warrant is the Word of God:
    Nought else is worth believing.

Though all my heart should feel condemned
    For want of some sweet token,
There is one greater than my heart
    Whose Word cannot be broken.

I'll trust in God's unchanging Word
    Till soul and body sever:
For, though all things shall pass away,
    His Word shall stand for ever.

Martin Luther

November 27
The apostle Peter gives this heartwarming
reassurance in chapter 1, verse 23, of his first letter.

"For you have been born again, not of perishable
seed, but of imperishable, through the living and
enduring word of God."

November 28
"Those who determine not to put self to death will never
see the will of God fulfilled in their lives. Those who ought
to become the light of the world must necessarily burn and
become less and less. By denying self we are able to win
others."

Sadhu Sundar Singh

November 29
"God weigheth more with how much love a man
worketh, than how much he doeth. He doeth much
that loveth much."

Thomas à Kempis

November 30
Today the people of Scotland
remember their patron saint, St. Andrew.

"As Jesus was walking beside the Sea of Galilee, he
saw two brothers, Simon called Peter and his brother
Andrew. They were casting a net into the lake, for
they were fishermen. 'Come, follow me,' Jesus said,
'and I will make you fishers of men.' At once they left
their nets and followed him."

Matthew 4:18-20

DECEMBER

December 1
"He who is filled with love is filled with God himself."
St. Augustine

December 2
St. Francis Xavier's feast day falls on December 2.
He once wrote, "Be great in little things."

December 3
"Go with each of us to rest; if any awake, temper to them the dark hours of watching; and when the day returns, return to us, our sun and comforter, and call us up with morning faces and with morning hearts, eager to labor, eager to be happy, if happiness should be our portion, and if the day be marked by sorrow, strong to endure it."

A prayer by Robert Louis Stevenson on the night before he died,
December 3, 1894

December 4

"Consider it pure joy, my brothers, whenever you face trials of many kinds, because you know that the testing of your faith develops perseverance. Perseverance must finish its work so that you may be mature and complete, not lacking anything."

James 1:2-4

December 5

Christina G. Rossetti, born on December 5, 1830, is one of England's best poets. In this verse from her carol *In the bleak midwinter*, she sums up our response to God's gift of Jesus.

> What can I give him,
> Poor as I am?
> If I were a shepherd,
> I would bring a lamb;
> If I were a wise man,
> I would do my part;
> Yet what I can I give him –
> Give my heart.

December 6

Lord Shaftesbury, the champion of the poor and down-trodden of the nineteenth century, lived by the following motto, which he wrote when he was twenty-seven:

"The first principle God's honor, the second man's happiness, the means prayer and unremitting diligence."

December 7

On Sunday, December 7, 1941, the United States naval base at Pearl Harbor in the Hawaiian Islands was attacked by nearly two hundred Japanese torpedo aircraft, bombers, and fighters.

"What causes wars, and what causes fightings among you? Is it not your passions that are at war in your members? You desire and you do not have; so you kill. And you covet and cannot obtain; so you fight and wage war."

James 4:1,2

December 8

"Naught but the name of Jesus can restrain the impulse of anger, repress the swelling of pride, cure the world of envy, bridle the onslaught of luxury, extinguish the flame of carnal desire – can temper avarice, and put to flight impure and ignoble thoughts."

Bernard of Clairvaux

December 9

"He who dwells in the shelter of the Most High
    will rest in the shadow of the Almighty.
I will say of the Lord, 'He is my refuge and my fortess,
    my God, in whom I trust.'"

Psalm 91:1,2

December 10

"When some men discharge an obligation,
you can hear the report for miles around."

Mark Twain

December 11

Jesus said, "When you give to the needy, do not announce it with trumpets, as the hypocrites do in the synagogues and on the streets, to be honored by men. I tell you the truth, they have received their reward in full. But when you give to the needy, do not let your left hand know what your right hand is doing, so that your giving may be in secret. Then your Father, who sees what is done in secret, will reward you."

Matthew 6:2-4

December 12

Now thank we all our God,
With hearts, and hands, and voices;
Who wondrous things has done,
In whom his world rejoices;
Who, from our mothers' arms,
Has blessed us on our way
With countless gifts of love,
And still is ours today.

Martin Rinkart

December 13

Bernard of Clairvaux wrote that there were three stages of growth in Christian maturity:

"Love of self for self's sake
Love of God for self's sake
Love of God for God"

December 14

Frances Ridley Havergal was born this day, 1836. When she was fifteen she dedicated herself to God and later wrote: "I committed my soul to the Savior, and earth and heaven seemed brighter from that moment."

December 15

Ought we not to be more thorough in our
service, not simply doing well that which
will be seen and noticed, but as our Father
makes many a flower to bloom unseen in the
lonely desert, so to do all we can do, as under
His eye, though no other eye can ever take
note of it?

Hudson Taylor

December 16

One of the leaders of the Pilgrim Fathers, William
Bradford, on arriving in America on December 16, 1620,
made this diary entry:

"Being thus arrived in a good harbor and brought
safe to land, they fell upon their knees and blessed
the God of Heaven, who had brought them over the
vast and furious ocean, and delivered them from
all the perils and miseries thereof."

December 17

"Behind every saint stands another saint. "

Friedrich von Hugel

December 18

On December 18, 1707, Charles Wesley was born.
He wrote this hymn for Christmas Day.

> Hark! The herald–angels sing,
> "Glory to the new–born King!
> Peace on earth, and mercy mild,
> God and sinners reconciled."
> Joyful, all you nations, rise,
> Join the triumph of the skies;
> With the angelic host proclaim:
> "Christ is born in Bethlehem!
> Hark! The herald–angels sing,
> "Glory to the new–born King!"

December 19

"Dear friends, do not be surprised at the painful
trial you are suffering, as though something strange
were happening to you. But rejoice that you
participate in the sufferings of Christ, so that you
may be overjoyed when his glory is revealed."

1 Peter 4:12,13

December 20

> Once in royal David's city,
> Stood a lowly cattle shed,
> Where a mother laid her baby,
> In a manger for his bed.
> Mary was that mother mild,
> Jesus Christ her little child.

C.F. Alexander

December 21

"There were only a few shepherds at the first
Bethlehem. The ox and the ass understood more
of the first Christmas than the high priests in
Jerusalem. And it is the same today."

Thomas Merton

December 22

The shepherds sing, and shall I be silent?
My God, no hymn for thee?
My soul's a shepherd too; a flock it feeds
Of thoughts and words and deeds:
The pasture of thy word; the streams of grace,
Enriching all the place.
Shepherds and flock shall sing, and all my powers
Out–sing the daylight hours.

George Herbert

December 23

There fared a mother driven forth
Out of an inn to roam;
In the place where she was homeless
All men are at home.
The crazy stable close at hand,
With shaking timber and shifting sand,
Grew a stronger thing to abide and stand
Then the square stones of Rome.

G.K. Chesterton

December 24

"Christ has no body now on earth but yours;
yours are the only hands with which he can do his
work,
yours are the only feet with which he can go about
the world,
yours are the only eyes through which his
compassion
can shine forth upon a troubled world.
Christ has no body now on earth but yours."

Teresa of Avila

December 25

"While Mary and Joseph were in Bethlehem,
the time came for the baby to be born,
and she gave birth to her firstborn, a son.
She wrapped him in cloths and placed him in a manger,
because there was no room for them in the inn."

Luke 2:6

December 26

Today is the day on which Stephen, the first
Christian martyr, is remembered.

"While they were stoning him, Stephen prayed,
'Lord Jesus, receive my spirit.' Then he fell on his knees and
cried out, 'Lord, do not hold this sin against them.' When he
had said this he fell asleep."

Acts 7:59,60

December 27

Innocents' Day falls today, commemorating
the moment when King Herod gave the orders
to kill all baby boys in and around Bethlehem
who were under the age of two.

"He who passively accepts evil is as much involved in it as he
who helps to perpetuate it."

Martin Luther King Jr.

December 28

December 28, 1944, is the date stamped
on Corrie ten Boom's release documents
from the Nazi concentration camp at
Ravensbruck. During her
imprisonment, and after it, she
aimed to live her life in the power
of God's Spirit. She wrote, "The
question on Pentecost is not
whether God is blessing our own
plans and program but whether
we are open to the great
opportunities to which his Spirit
calls us."

December 29

David Livingstone was once asked if he didn't fear that going into Africa was too difficult and too dangerous and he replied, "I am immortal until the will of God for me is accomplished."

December 30

"It is our care for the helpless, our practise of lovingkindness, that brands us in the eyes of many of our opponents. 'Look!' they say. 'How they love one another! Look how they are prepared to die for one another.'"

Tertullian

December 31

"And I said to the man who stood at the gate of the year: 'Give me a light that I may tread safely into the unknown!'"

"And he replied: 'Go out into the darkness and put thine hand into the Hand of God. That shall be to thee better than light and safer than a known way.'"

"So I went forth and finding the Hand of God trod gladly into the night."

M.L. Haskins